Car badges

i-SPY

ID0656771

INTRODUCTION

Almost all cars – as well as vans, lorries and buses – carry a logo that lets you know which company made them. The usual positions for this are on the front 'grille' (the slatted opening that allows air in to cool the engine's radiator) or else on the bonnet. Most cars feature their logo on the back too, generally situated above the number plate.

On any car journey – or on a walk along a busy road, or through a car park – you might come across dozens of these little symbols. But what, exactly, do they all mean? Why is there a three-pointed star on Mercedes-Benz cars, or a lion on MAN trucks, or two little chevrons on Citroën vans? This i-SPY book tries to explain these marques. It helps you have fun on any journey by explaining many of the car brands you're likely to come across on British roads. As there have been more than 6500 different makes of car and commercial vehicle since 1885, we couldn't possibly include every one. But we have included the logo of most brands currently on UK sale (plus a few that are common in other countries, and might be seen here occasionally), and several from classic marques which, while no longer manufactured, are still relatively common sights. It's quite difficult to spy some of the rarer car logos, because they are found on expensive sports and luxury cars of which only a handful are sold in Britain each year. On the other hand, we've also included the logos found on most of the commercial vehicles you'll come across. Don't pass a truck or bus without trying to see if it could earn you i-SPY points!

By getting to know car logos, you'll understand more about the people who founded each car manufacturer, the places they come from, and sometimes the company's achievements or ambitions. If you thought logos were only found on clothes, electronic gadgets and food packaging then you're in for a few surprises!

How to use your i-SPY book

We've selected these logos to reflect the widest possible range of cars and commercial vehicles you're likely to spy across Britain. They're arranged in alphabetical order, so you may need to memorise the logo as you hunt through the book to identify it if the make is not obvious from the badge. You need 1000 points to send off for your i-SPY certificate (see page 64) but that is not too difficult because there are masses of points in every book. Each entry has a star or circle and points value beside it. The stars represent harder to spot entries. As you make each i-SPY, write your score in the circle or star.

Points: 25

You will find this image of an aggressive scorpion on high performance Fiats. Karl Abarth was an Austrian speed addict who first built racing cars and equipment in Italy in 1949. Fiat took over his firm in 1971. Abarth's star sign was Scorpio, hence the scorpion.

AC

Top Spot! Points: 40

The initials stand for Auto Carriers, as the company now known for high-performance sports cars like the 1963 Cobra originally built three-wheeled Auto Carrier delivery trucks! When it moved into cars, the curved 'A' and 'C' were cast into the wheel hubs. Framed in a circle from 1925, they made a neat badge.

Points: 35

AIXAM

This is a French brand of ultra-small city cars that, in some cases, can be driven without a full driver's licence. Aixam's logo used to be a 'M' with a pair of wings, but this has recently been replaced by an 'A' and the company name.

meunierd / Shutterstock.com

The coat of arms of the Italian city of Milan, where Alfa Romeo was founded in 1910, is the centrepiece. The red cross on the left salutes the local army's earliest crusade of 1095. The green serpent on the right dates back to the sixth century, when Germanic tribes conquered northern Italy; look closely and you will see that the beast is eating its foe – a man!

ALPINA

Points: 30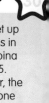

Burkard Bovensiepen set up his BMW tuning business in an outbuilding of the Alpina typewriter factory in 1965. More than 50 years later, the typewriter firm is long gone and Alpina is offering high-performance versions of current BMWs while older Alpina BMWs are collectors' items. The badge wraps the name around what looks like a heraldic crest but is actually a Weber carburettor and a crankshaft on a shield.

All Alvis cars, carefully hand-built in Coventry, had this red triangle badge on their radiator shells between 1922 and 1967. Over 4300 of them survive. The name derives from the Aluminum Alloy Pistons company, and was chosen because it sounded good in any language. In 2010, the name was revived on 'continuation' versions of 1930s and 1960s models.

The capital 'A' depicted in the Ariel's badge is designed to look like a road stretching into the distance. This high-powered, two-seater fun car, which is built in a small factory in Somerset, is unusual in having no conventional bodywork; the chassis and frame of the car are fully exposed, while the mid-mounted engine comes from the Honda Civic Type-R. In 2015, Ariel launched an off-road buggy called the Nomad.

ASTON MARTIN

Points: 30

Aston Martins have featured a 'winged' motif since 1932. It represents a scarab beetle in flight, wings outstretched, and reflects the 1930s craze for Egyptology. The company's title unites the name of co-founder Lionel Martin, with Aston Clinton, the Buckinghamshire village where it had great success in the hill climb competition up nearby Aston Hill.

 Points: 10

AUDI

The four interlinked rings of the Audi logo are a neat pointer to the company's quattro four-wheel drive system. But it actually originated in 1932, when four German carmakers – Audi, DKW, Horch and Wanderer – merged.

AUSTIN

Points: 25

Austins were popular British family cars built between 1905 and 1988. This motif from a 1950s Austin A90 Atlantic, shows a 3D wheel with wings, above the scripted name and coat of arms of the founder Herbert Austin. Other models only show one or two of these individual items in the badge. Score for any Austin badge.

Points: 35

Austin-Healeys are some of the best-loved classic British sports cars, even though the last one was sold in 1971. The Austin and Healey companies joined forces to launch their first two-seater roadster in 1952. The logo they created for it followed others in framing the words with stylised bird's wing emblems to suggest swiftness. Differing slightly on each model, the logo generally features red enamel on a chrome base.

Martin Charles Hatch / Shutterstock.com

Points: 50   **Top Spot!**

BAC

The Briggs Automotive Company is based in Speke, Liverpool, and makes only one car: the Mono. It's a highly specialised single-seat road car launched in 2011 and set up to be as close to a racing single-seater as possible. Power comes from a 285bhp Cosworth four-cylinder engine and the gearbox is a Hewland six-speed unit from a Formula 3 car. The badge is as minimal as the car: just a decal to save weight.

Andrew Lofthouse

BENTLEY

Points: 30

One of the most elegant 'winged' badges you'll see on any car adorns the radiator grilles of Bentleys. On older cars, and some newer ones, you'll also see a three-dimensional Bentley mascot featuring a capital 'B' with wings outstretched behind it.

 Points: 30

BERTONE

Bertone isn't a make of car but an Italian company which designs and assembles cars for other companies. You might spot it on lots of cars ranging from older Vauxhaul Astra coupés to the classic Lamborghini Countach!

BMW

Points: 5

BMW stands for Bayerische Motoren Werke or, in English, the Bavarian Motor Works. Before it started car-making in 1928 it was famous for its aeroplane engines.The centre of the logo resembles a spinning propeller in the colours of the Bavarian flag.

Brabus is an aftermarket tuning company famous for their often outrageous power upgrades to Mercedes-Benz cars, from the giant G-wagen off-roader to the tiny Smart ForTwo. The name comes from the first three letters of the founders' surnames, BRA-ckman and BUS-chmann, and the circled B on the bonnet or boot lid is usually complemented by the company name in extra-bold block capitals.

The logo for these expensive British cars features the Bristol coat of arms because the cars were hand-built in the West Country city. It's a shield showing a castle on a clifftop with, on the horizon, a ship sailing into port. The '2 LITRE' part of the logo was dropped in 1961 when the company started using larger American V8 engines. Production ceased in 2011 when the firm changed hands but a new model is in development.

In March 2016 Bugatti revealed the Chiron, the latest in their range of supercars. It is built for speed with acceleration of 0–62mph in 2.5 seconds and a limited top speed of 261mph. The Bugatti emblem on the Chiron's radiator grille is a third larger than its predecessor was and is the only component of the Chiron that has not been subjected to the painstaking weight saving programme around the car's development. At 26cm wide, hand-crafted from silver and enamel, its 3-D design creates the effect of letters hovering over the red enamel. Ettore Bugatti's motto was "nothing is too beautiful and nothing is too expensive."

Buicks are traditional American cars, which means they tend to be large, powerful and luxurious. Buick used a single shield as a grille badge from 1937, changing to this 'Trishield' in 1960. A Buick Hawk badge took over in the 1970s but the Trishield returned in the 1980s. It was very loosely adapted from the family crest of David Buick, the company's Scottish founder.

CADILLAC

Points: 35

Frenchman Antoine de la Mothe Cadillac founded the American city of Detroit in 1701. The place would become the centre of US car-making in the 20th century, and one of its most famous marques adopted not only Cadillac's name but also, for its logo, his family crest. American presidents have traditionally used Cadillacs as official transport, but only small numbers are sold in the UK.

Points: 35

Caterham's sports cars have been adored by keen drivers since 1973, when the Caterham, Surrey based company bought the design rights to the two-seater Super Seven from Lotus. Lotus's own logo was adapted by upturning the familiar camshaft lobe shape. Inside this, the word 'SUPER' was arrayed above the figure '7' on a bright yellow background. The usual colour scheme is yellow and green on chrome.

Points: 20

The logo for this US-originated car brand is nicknamed the 'bowtie'. Louis Chevrolet was a Swiss racing driver, but it was businessman William Durant who made the company successful. He used to tell the tale that he noticed the bowtie shape on wallpaper in a Paris hotel, but in fact he copied it from the trademark for Coalette firelighters that he spotted in a newspaper advert!

tovtdo / Shutterstock.com

Points: 15

The elaborate, old-fashioned logo for America's Chrysler cars was the idea of Walter Chrysler himself. He wanted it to look like the kind of rosette that might be seen pinned to prize-winning livestock because, when he started his firm in 1923, he thought that wealthy farmers were the best customers to target. The logo was dropped in 1962 but revived in 1998.

CITROËN

Points: 10

Citroën enthusiasts call this logo the 'double chevron'. It represents the precision-machined grooves on gear wheels, as these are what André Citroën manufactured before expanding into cars in 1919; Citroën gears were even fitted to the ill-fated liner Titanic. The double chevron is expressed in various ways on Citroën vehicles, though the separate DS brand of premium Citroen models has dropped the double chevron entirely.

Since 2013, when the Renault owned Dacia company started marketing strongly into the UK, the badge has become a familiar site on Britain's roads. Models include the Sandero, Logan and Duster.

Points: 20 20

DAEWOO

It is pronounced 'Day-oo' and means, in Korean, 'the great universe'. Daewoos were sold in the UK between 1995 and 2004 – budget-priced family cars from South Korea.

DAF

Points: 10 10

There are many DAF trucks on UK roads as they have a factory in Leyland, Lancashire. The letters stand for Doorne's Aanhangwagen Fabriek which, translated from the original Dutch, means Doorne's Trailer Factory.

Points: 15

Daihatsu is one of Japan's smaller carmakers, although it has links to Toyota. Its cars are 'niche' products like city cars, sports cars, 4x4 off-roaders and small delivery vans. It has a bold and simple logo, a capital 'D' tilted to the left and usually displayed in an oval frame. The word Daihatsu is a compound of the Japanese words for 'Osaka', where it is based, and 'motor'.

Points: 20

This is the oldest British car marque, having been founded in 1896 as a branch of the German Daimler company. Yet the stylish logo you see here wasn't attached to a Daimler until 1960; before that time, the cars didn't have one at all, and were identifiable only by their fluted radiator grille frame. Daimlers became re-badged Jaguars; the last was sold in the UK in 2008.

DE TOMASO

The blue and white striped background to the De Tomaso logo is the Argentine flag and the black 'T' shape symbolises a branding iron. It salutes the ancestry of Alejandro de Tomaso's family as cattle ranchers in the Andes. Built in Modena, Italy, these cars are known for being rare, fast and beautiful machines. Very few have been made since 1990, so they're an unusual spot on UK roads.

 Points: 20

DODGE

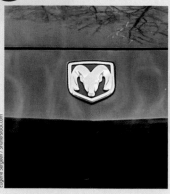

This evocation of a bighorn ram was first seen on Dodge vehicles in 1932, shortly after Walter Chrysler took control of the American make. He liked the way the 'king of the trail' animal summed up toughness. After a period in the wilderness, the ram livery returned to Dodges from the early 1990s, and today you will find it on all its cars and pick-up trucks.

Eugene Sergeev / Shutterstock.com

In a British poll conducted in 2009, Ferrari's prancing black horse logo was voted the 'most iconic' in the world. It first appeared as a lucky charm on the side of Enzo Ferrari's race team cars in the 1930s. The bright yellow is the traditional colour for Modena, where the cars are built. On Ferrari competition cars, the initials 'SF' are sometimes added; they stand for 'Scuderia Ferrari', meaning 'Team Ferrari'.

Radu Bercan / Shutterstock.com

Fiat has changed the logo on its cars many times over the years, and the very latest one is actually a return to a design used between 1959 and 1966. One feature, however, has remained pretty much intact since 1901, and that is the unique capital 'A' with the right-hand stem kinked inwards. Fiat is actually an acronym, standing for Fabbrica Italiana Automobili Torino (Italian Automobile Factory of Turin).

Points: 20

For 150 years between 1856 and 2006, Cheshire-based Foden made working machines for British business, first steam engines and then trucks. Although no longer manufactured, there are still plenty of large Foden vehicles on British roads, with their flowing 'Foden' script in a four-pointed star as a logo on the front. They are generally articulated trucks or eight-wheel tippers.

Points: 5

Often referred to as the 'blue oval', the Ford logo is one of the most familiar in Britain, as its cars and vans have been best-sellers here for decades. The curly, silver script was designed by Childe Harold Wills, an assistant to Henry Ford, in 1903. He used a home printing press he had in his attic . . . the same machine he had used as a teenager to make pocket money by printing and selling calling cards to friends and neighbours.

Points: 15 15

You will find this little emblem on the side window pillars of the top luxury model in most Ford ranges. The lettering is a rendering of the signature of Italian car bodywork designer Giacinto Ghia. From 1919, his company was renowned for its stylish coachwork – most famously for the Volkswagen Karmann-Ghia. Ford bought the design house in 1973, and used the trademark on its cars until 2010.

Points: 40   **Top Spot!**

Ginetta is one of several small British sports car manufacturers, and its many different models of two-seaters have been popular with road and track drivers since it opened for business in 1958.The triangulated 'G' on a yellow circle makes for a simple logo, but a mystery remains. The four Walklett brothers who started the company have never revealed where the inspiration for the Ginetta name came from.

★ **Points: 50**   **Top Spot!**

Only 99 of these fast, Corvette-engined GT cars were made before the Southampton-based company went bust in 1966, but most survive and they're now highly sought-after. The badge was an idea from Jim Keeble, the engineer behind the marque: a pet tortoise walked out from under a hedge during a photoshoot with the prototype. Keeble decided it was perfect: 'very steady on its pins, you never see one on its roof, so we'll go for the opposite of things like a Jaguar or a prancing horse.'

HONDA

Nui2013 / Shutterstock.com

The prominent 'H' on the front of all Hondas means there's no mistaking any of its cars. The uprights of the 'H' are splayed out slightly, and it is sometimes displayed on a red background, although mostly it uses a black one. The popular Civic, Jazz and CR-V are all British made. Honda motorbikes have a different logo, featuring a large, single bird's wing above the word 'HONDA'.

Points: 35

The massive Hummer off-roaders don't have a logo as such; the tough, high-riding sport-utility vehicles simply spell out the marque name on the front in heavy-set capital letters. The Hummer is derived from an American military vehicle, the High Mobility Multipurpose Wheeled Vehicle – commonly known as the 'Humvee'.

Points: 10

In contrast to Honda, Hyundai uses a strange slanted 'H' on the front of its cars, worn as an entirely chrome decoration. It was first seen in 1991. Hyundais come from South Korea, where they have been produced since 1974, and have been sold in the UK since 1982. The range today spans everything from city cars to large people carriers, and most things in between.

Points: 20

Infiniti cars are becoming almost as common in the UK as they are in the USA, where they've been sold since 1989. They are not, in fact, American but a range of sports and luxury models built by Nissan in Japan.

Points: 20

Isuzu is one of Japan's smaller manufacturers, concentrating on pick-up trucks and 4x4 vehicles. They also make larger delivery trucks that are popular in the UK. Isuzu vehicles carry the company name as a badge, usually on the radiator grille.

Points: 10

Vans and trucks made by IVECO are a common sight in this country. Although the Industrial Vehicle Corporation, which is shortened to IVECO, is part of the Italian Fiat organisation, it has factories all over Europe. It has no logo other than the spelling of its name, which sits boldly on the front of its trucks, vans and minibuses.

The statuette of a pouncing jaguar is known, in Jaguar circles, as 'the leaper'. It has been used since 1938 when S.S. Cars (later Jaguar) offered it as a radiator mascot. Most Jaguars also sport a bonnet badge showing the growling face of the big cat from South America. The leaper has not been standard on Jaguars since 2005 due to safety concerns in frontal collisions.

The first Jeep was a lightweight four-wheel drive military vehicle. The name, really a nickname, probably derives from the US Army abbreviation GP, for 'general purpose', and/or from a cartoon character called Eugene the Jeep. Willys-Overland trademarked it in 1950 and the brand survives to this day, now used by Fiat Chrysler Automobiles on a range of four-wheel drive SUVs and off-roaders.

Points: 30

Jensen's most famous car was the Interceptor, a four-seater luxury model introduced in 1966 and winning admiration for its Aston Martin-like image and performance. The Jensen logo was another winged wonder. You also score if you see the more intricate 'wing' logo on earlier Jensens like the C-V8 or 541.

Points: 25

Keep a sharp eye out for the shield-shaped logo of German coachbuilder Karmann. The firm builds convertible cars for large car companies, but you will only see this logo on convertible Renaults like the 19 and the last two generations of Megane. Karmann's open-top version of the Volkswagen Golf also has it moulded into the roll-over frame, but the classic Karmann Ghia features only 'KARMANN' wording.

Points: 10

Kia has been selling more and more cars to British drivers, especially since the South Korean manufacturers opened a European plant in Slovakia. The current oval Kia logo has graced all its cars since 1996. In raised chrome with a black background, it features an unusual capital 'A' that does without the usual crossbar.

Goran Bogicevic / Shutterstock.com

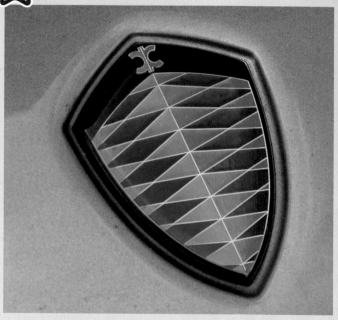

Christian von Koenigsegg was just 22 when he decided to build a Swedish supercar that would compete with Ferrari. It took him eight years but, in 2002, the amazing, 240mph Koenigsegg CC8S was launched to rave reviews. Just a handful have been sold in the UK, but if you see one it will bear this logo on the front. It is Christian's own interpretation of the von Koenigsegg family crest, which dates back to the 16th century.

LADA

Russia's gigantic Lada factory, 600 miles southeast of Moscow, doesn't export many of its cars to the West any more; when it did, they found a ready market because they were robust and cheap. The Viking longboat image on the cars' logo commemorates the fact that there was once a Norse invasion in the region the factory occupies. Few British-registered Ladas have escaped the crusher.

LAGONDA

Top Spot! **Points: 45**

Lagonda was a British luxury carmaker established way back in 1906 and taken over in 1947 by David Brown, then owner of Aston Martin. It produced luxury saloons alongside Aston's sportier GT cars until 1989 but has now been revived with the new £700,000 Taraf model. The badge, similar to Aston Martin's, was winged long before the companies were merged You can score for absolutely any Lagonda you encounter!

meunierd / Shutterstock.com

Millionaire industrialist Ferruccio Lamborghini, it is said, vowed to make better supercars than Ferrari and – with the stunning Lamborghini Miura, Countach, Diablo and Gallardo – the two marques are certainly neck-and-neck for driving excitement.

Lambo's logo sought to outdo Ferrari too, with a charging bull instead of Ferrari's bucking stallion. Signor Lamborghini chose this because he was born under the star sign of Taurus, for the bull.

Lancia's shield-shaped logo has been around as long as the upmarket Italian cars themselves – that is, since 1908. So has the dark blue colour and the suggestion of a steering wheel. Lancia has built some fantastic cars in its 100-plus years – including the rally-winning Delta Integrale – but they are not currently sold in the UK, so hard to spot.

LAND ROVER

Points: 10

First revealed in 1948, the four-wheel drive Land Rover has always featured an oval logo with the 'LAND' and 'ROVER' words linked by a zig-zag hyphen. Oddly, the marque has never used a hyphen on its title but, until 1984, its vehicle badging did have one. The Land Rover logo today is always seen in green with cream lettering, zigzag and outline.

Points: 15

LDV

LDVs are small- to medium-sized delivery vans and pick-up trucks that are widely used all over Britain. The letters stand for Leyland DAF Vans, as the Birmingham manufacturer was once part of DAF and, before that, British Leyland. Sadly, in the recession of 2009, LDV closed down, but a Chinese firm, SAIC, bought the name and is launching four new LDV vans in the UK.

Top Spot! **Points: 45**

45

Lea-Francis started building cars under its own name in 1919 but by 1954 they were out of business, reviving sporadically in 1960 and 1998. The badge features the initials of founders Richard Lea and Graham Francis but also a strange creature called a unihorse – half a unicorn and half a seahorse. Although 'half a unicorn and half a fish' might be more accurate, and the reasons for using it on a radiator badge are obscure.

15 **Points: 15**

According to Lexus, the Japanese luxury car marque, the logo 'signifies the company's ever-expanding technological advancement and the limitless opportunities which lie ahead'. That is the message behind what most people would describe as a large capital 'L' framed by an ellipse. Lexus cars are actually made by Toyota, which launched this high-end brand in 1989 to match BMW, Mercedes-Benz and Jaguar for comfort and style.

Founded in 1920 and named after American president Abraham Lincoln, this is Ford's luxury car division. Its large, impressive products are very rarely found outside the USA, so you will be lucky to see one on British roads. Lincolns first boasted a heraldic crest in 1942, although it was totally made up by Ford's graphic designers. The only part of that crest that remains today is a four-pointed star, set across a four-sided shape.

Points: 25

The Lotus logo, always presented in a yellow circle, is a green, vaguely triangular shape that looks like a camshaft lobe in a high-performance engine. It always carries a monogram at the top above the 'LOTUS' name; this combination of A, C, B and C stands for Anthony Colin Bruce Chapman, the man who founded the Norfolk sports carmaker back in 1947.

LTC stands for the London Taxi Company, now Chinese-owned, who build the iconic Black Cabs of London. The current model is known as the TX4, and is the latest in a long line of taxis made by LTC and its forerunners specially designed to cope with London's narrow streets and vast area.

The animal depicted in the logo on MAN trucks is the Büssing lion. It's used because MAN took over a rival truck-maker in 1971 and adopted their lion badge. MAN stands for 'Maschinenfabrik Augsburg Nürnberg', or the Machinery Factories of Augsburg & Nürnberg.

Corporate MAN

With the word 'MARCOS' in a blue oval at its centre, a contrasting, diagonal red stripe, and the background as a white flash, the Marcos logo makes an impact and signifies the fact these rare classic sports cars are thoroughly British. Although not currently being manufactured, they have been road and track favourites since 1959.

Sergey Kohl / Shutterstock.com

nanhatai / Shutterstock.com

Neptune, the legendary nautical god, brandished his three-pronged trident to command the waves. There is a bronze sculpture of him in a fountain in Bologna's Piazza Del Nettuno, and this inspired the Maserati brothers to adopt the trident as their logo back in 1926. It has been found on Maserati cars ever since, and features on the front, back and sides of today's GranTurismo, Ghibli and Quattroporte models.

The Maybach 57 and 62 were created by Mercedes-Benz in 2002 as the epitome in super-luxury limousines. They are often owned by celebrities. On their imposing bonnets, under which reside powerful V12 engines, they carry a three-dimensional version of the Maybach logo, which consists of two inter-linked capital 'M's. They stand for 'Maybach Manufaktur'. The original Maybach was built between 1921 and 1940.

10 **Points: 10**

The V-shape in the middle of Mazda's logo spreads out like an opening fan, representing, the Japanese company says, 'the creativity, the sense of mission, the resoluteness and vitality of Mazda'. Poised like wings ready to fly, the 'V' is also a 'starting point for future growth'. It was introduced in 1997, so older Mazdas carry different symbols; score for any that you spy.

McLaren has been most well known, until now, for its Formula 1 racing team – a mainstay of the sport for decades. It also made the rare 231mph F1 road car in 1993. But the Woking-based company is now taking on Ferrari, Lamborghini and Porsche with its mid-engined 540C, 570S, 650S and the amazing P1 hypercar. Score for any version of the boomerang-like 'speedmark' logo shown here at the end of the name.

Points: 10

MERCEDES-BENZ

Rodu Bercan / Shutterstock.com

The three-pointed star emblem has been a design feature on Mercedes-Benz cars and trucks since about 1910. Today, you will find it as a freestanding bonnet ornament, a large chrome cut-out, and as an enamel badge picked out in blue with a laurel wreath around its edge. The three points symbolise air, water and land, the three transport areas for which the company made engines in its early days.

MERCURY

Top Spot!   **Points: 40**

40

You are not going to see many Mercury cars in the UK, as they have never been sold here; any that have crept in will be personal imports or, possibly, owned by US military personnel. In the USA, though, they are a popular, sporty line of cars made and sold by Ford. Since 1985, Mercurys have carried this logo showing the three stems of a capital 'M'.

MG stands for Morris Garages, the sales network of Oxford-based carmaker Morris that came up with the idea for an affordable sports car using existing Morris parts. The distinctive, octagonal logo was created by MG accountant Edmund Lee, a talented amateur artist, in 1923. It first appeared on a car in 1928, and its traditional colour scheme is brown on cream. MG is now Chinese-owned.

Points: 10

A prominent chrome 'MINI' set against a black circle, with four chrome bars descending in size to form the simple wings either side make up this typically British car logo, ironically now seen on the modern BMW-owned Mini models. The original was launched as both an Austin and a Morris in 1959 before Mini became its own marque in 1969.

Points: 15

This trademark first appeared in the 1870s on a Japanese ship owned by Yataro Iwasaki. He used it to honour his mentors, the powerful Toso clan, whose family crest contained three oak leaves. Iwasaki's own crest included three stacked diamonds, and the whole resembled a ship's three-bladed propeller. Mitsubishi is Japanese for 'three diamonds'. The company part-founded Japan's NYK shipping line, and diversified into cars in 1960.

Points: 30

MORGAN

The Morgan 4/4 is the longest surviving car model ever. First introduced in 1936, you can still buy one in 2016! The logo has also sailed through these 80 years pretty much untouched. 'MORGAN' sits on a black cross as a centrepiece, with an elaborate plumage of wings outstretched behind it. Morgans are sports cars hand-built in Malvern, Worcester.

Points: 30

This logo features an ox crossing a ford, apparently hinting at the British city from which the cars hailed. It was actually taken from Oxford's coat of arms. Indeed, the Morris Oxford was a popular model, but you are most likely to see the logo on the many Morris Minors still in everyday use – it was the first British car to reach a million sales. The last new Morris was sold in 1984.

Points: 10

The 'NISSAN' name in black capitals appears in a bar set across a circle and, on the car, the whole logo is reproduced in chrome. It is a little similar to the style of station signs on the London Underground. The logo derives from the early Nissan corporate identity that showed the circle in red, to signify Japan's national motto of being 'the land of the rising sun'.

Sergey Kohl / Shutterstock.com

There is a slim chance you might see one of these large American cars on a British street, but you will definitely see plenty in the USA because, between 1901 and 2004, over 35 million Oldsmobiles were sold. General Motors finally decided to axe the brand because Americans found it old-fashioned and dull. A range of badges were used over the years but most versions of the logo included a stylized image of a rocket on take-off.

Points: 25

Opel is the brand name used all over Europe by General Motors – in fact, everywhere except the UK, where the same cars are sold as Vauxhall. The chrome logo consists of a lightning flash across a circle; it dates back to 1962 when the previous logo, showing a torpedo flashing across a circle, was updated. A small number of Opels do end up in Britain, so look out for them.

Top Spot!   **Points: 50**

This cast metal logo is found on the exotic Pagani supercars that come from Modena in Italy. Horacio Pagani is the man behind these hugely fast and powerful two-seaters that compete with Ferraris and Lamborghinis. Pagani only builds a few dozen cars annually whereas Ferrari manufacture is in the thousands. The Huayra, the company's latest supercar, cost a staggering £1.4 million – but by February 2015 it had sold out.

aGinger / Shutterstock.com

The intricate wire mesh grille usually found on pre-war British sports cars forms the main part of the Panther logo, along with the traditional 'winged' element. Panthers were made between 1972 and 1990, and were usually entirely styled along the lines of 1930s models. They are all pretty rare but you might see one of the Vauxhall-engined Limas or Ford-powered Kallistas, perhaps at a classic car show.

Points: 20

The elliptical logo on this range of economy cars imported from Malaysia is split diagonally across the centre, sometimes into green and red sections. The chrome divider suggests the silhouette of a capital 'P'; however, it is just possible to visualise it as the profile of a leaping deer, as this was what formed the Perodua logo until 2000. The company ceased UK imports after 2013 due to poor sales.

Points: 10

Peugeot started making cutting implements in 1810. It was in 1858 that the badge motif started to adorn their products to show the products strength through the lion logo. Vehicle production started in 1889 and Peugeot cars have been stamped with the lion ever since.

Here is another logo belonging not to a manufacturer but a car design company. Italy's Pininfarina styles and assembles cars for other companies, lately including Ferrari, Peugeot, Alfa Romeo and Volvo. It was founded by Battista 'Pinin' Farina. He changed his name in 1961, combining nickname and surname, but Pininfarina-designed and/or -built cars often carry a blue and red 'f' crest above the distinctive Pininfarina script.

Points: 40 **Top Spot!**

Between 1928 and 2001, Plymouth was a sister car marque to Chrysler, named after the departure point of English pilgrims who were first to colonise North America. That is why the early logo, which was reintroduced for the last six years of Plymouth's existence, features the pilgrims' ship, the Mayflower. There are a few Plymouths in the UK, mostly older models owned by American classic car fanatics. Score for any Plymouth you see.

Pontiac is yet another American make of car recently made obsolete. General Motors decided to give Pontiac the chop in 2009 after 83 years. Its logo was a silver star on a red arrowhead. It was used to commemorate the chief of the Ottawa Indians, who led the rebellion against British settlers in 1763. Pontiac built some cool cars, but few were sold in the UK.

Points: 25

Like its sports car rival Ferrari, Porsche also features a prancing black horse in its logo. That is because it is a central component of the Stuttgart city coat of arms from which the logo draws heavily. In the Middle Ages, Stuttgart was the site of a stud farm (that is what the word actually means in German). The 'PORSCHE' name, in square-cut capitals, is familiar on the cars too.

chamsin / Shutterstock.com

The tiger is the national animal of Malaysia in much the same way that the bulldog is for Britain. As Protons are Malaysian-built, they sport a tiger's head motif on their logos. Original blue, green and gold colour ed badges have been replaced with a silver and black version on recent models.

 Points: 30

Reliant had a very unusual model range: they produced popular three-wheeled economy cars, notably the Regal and the Robin, but also a much larger, faster model; first the Sabre and then the Scimitar, a kind of sports estate car. The latter's badge featured the curved sword on a shield.

The large chrome diamond on all Renault cars, vans and trucks is easy to spot. A diamond-shaped emblem, originally with the word 'RENAULT' set across it, first appeared in 1925. At that time, Renaults were unusual in not having a traditional radiator grille, but the diamond-framed opening in the cars' nose panel acted as an outlet for the sound of the innovative electric horn behind it.

Points: 30

You are more likely to see this emblem, an 'R' in a circle, in London than anywhere else in Britain. That's because it is on the front of the Indian-made Reva G-Wiz electric car, a tiny two-seater that's been very popular with London residents and commuters because it emits zero emissions and benefits from free parking and no Congestion Charge fees.

Silvia Pascual / Shutterstock.com

The double 'R's in a rectangle celebrate the partnership between engineer Henry Royce and businessman Charles Rolls. It eventually led to both luxurious and expensive Rolls-Royce cars and some of the world's best aircraft engines. Up to 1930, the logo was always red-on-chrome, whereupon it was changed to black; however, red is sometimes used for limited edition cars. The Rolls-Royce radiator mascot is officially called 'The Spirit of Ecstasy'.

Points: 20

It was a sad day for British car enthusiasts when Rover ceased trading in 2005, ending 101 years of car-making, and closing the company's 100-year-old Longbridge factory. It also meant goodbye to Rover's logo, a front-on representation of a Viking longship with a Viking warrior figurehead on its prow.

Points: 15

Saab used to have an aeroplane on its badge, but in 1987 it was changed to match that of Scania (see below), as the two brands were part of the same company. Sadly, Saab ceased trading in 2011 and despite Chinese-backed revival attempts, it remains defunct.

Points: 15

This is a large commercial vehicle company, that builds a range of heavy trucks and chassis for coaches, so you are most likely to see Scanias on the motorway. The griffin, half lion and half eagle, comes from the crest for the Skåne province of southern Sweden, where Scania was founded although after a merger the company is now based in the more northerly province of Södermanland.

You pronounce it "Say-at" but the word actually stands for Sociedad Española de Automoviles de Turismo, or the Spanish Passenger Car Company. This style of distinctive capital 'S' as a logo has been around since 1998, and you will generally see it as a large, chrome emblem bordered in black. Seat is the biggest carmaker in Spain, where it was established in 1953 initially with the assistance of Fiat, but is today part of Volkswagen.

 Points: 20

These trucks have been around since 1970, when the rival Seddon and Atkinson truck-making firms in Lancashire merged. It was the Atkinson logo that won through, though – a big capital 'A' framed in a circle. The company is now part of IVECO and its UK plant shut down, but the brand name lives on. It is usually found on specialist vehicles for local councils, like refuse collectors.

Points: 10 10

If it wasn't for the familiarity of its name, this would be one of the most unusual logos you'd find on any car. First registered in 1924, it is actually supposed to show the feathers of an American Indian's headdress, along with an arrow. It hints at the fact that Škoda, based in the Czech Republic, originally made armaments. The 'eye' on the feathers was added to suggest vision.

20 **Points: 20** SMART

The Smart car first came along in 1997 as a joint venture between the company that created the Swatch watch and Daimler-Benz. Their concept was to produce an extremely short, economical and stylish city runabout. The current logo first appeared in 2002. It's a so-called 'pictogram' of a circle whose right-hand side is formed of a triangular arrow pointing outwards, and on the cars themselves it has a brushed aluminium finish.

Dong liu / Shutterstock.com

The exclusive Spyker C8 sports car, built in the Netherlands, was unveiled in 2000, but the make's first era of car-making was between 1900 and 1925. In those days, Spyker was also in the aeroplane business, and hence the logo mixes an aircraft propeller and a spoked car wheel. Arrayed around the lower part of the wheel is Spyker's Latin motto: NULLA TENACI INVIA EST VIA – for the tenacious, no road is impassable.

Points: 20

SSANGYONG

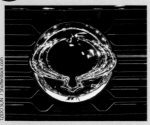

TZIDO SUN / Shutterstock.com

SsangYong means two dragons, and these are apparently represented in this logo. Korean legend has it that two dragons wanted to return to the skies but the 'skymaster' would only admit one of them. They refused to be parted and so agreed neither would enter. Suitably impressed, the skymaster relented and let them both in. South Korea's SsangYong offers the Korando, Tivoli, Rexton and Turismo models in the UK.

Subaru's logo is an oval with six, four-pointed stars inside it, one large one to the left and five smaller, identically-sized ones to the right. It has special resonance in Japan because it symbolises the star cluster Pleiades, in the Taurus constellation, which is a traditional feature in Japanese culture and literature. Indeed, 'subaru' means six stars in modern-day Japanese.

Points: 15

SUZUKI

Suzuki's spiky, compressed rendering of a capital 'S', in three parallel strokes, simply stands for Suzuki – that's as complex as it gets! The Suzuki Motor Corporation grew out of a family-owned loom-making business before diversifying into cars and motorbikes. Suzuki is one of the most common surnames in the Kanto region of Japan, which includes Tokyo, and the company is still controlled by the founding Suzuki family.

A capital 'T' in a circle – generally used as a plastic, silver-on-black radiator grille badge – means you've just spied a Talbot. It's likely to be a rare sight. Although the name dates back to the Earl of Shrewsbury & Talbot's car-making activities in 1903, it was revived between 1979 and 1986. Those 1980s Talbots like the Horizon and Samba sold badly, and most by now have gone to the scrapyard.

Points: 30

The Tata Nano grabbed headlines with its extraordinary price of just £1300 (in India, anyway) back in 2009 but somehow failed to catch on - a zero-stars score in crash testing didn't help. The logo looks like a chrome T-junction and you might see one on the handful of Tata's big, tough pick-ups in the UK.

Amnarj Tanongratana / Shutterstock.com

Top Spot! **Points: 45**

Tatra, of the Czech Republic, once made the innovative luxury cars that the country's leaders rode around in when the country was under Russian communist control. Today, though, the firm is known internationally for its range of trucks that feature traction to every wheel. The big, red and silver logo is most familiar in central Europe, so over here you're most likely to spot one at a classic car show.

Points: 30

TESLA

360b / Shutterstock.com

Tesla is the brainchild of PayPal co-founder and billionaire Elon Musk, and has moved from making a Lotus-like electric sports car to a high-quality luxury saloon, the Model S, that's added much credibility to the idea of electric cars. Serbian-born Nikola Tesla, who died in 1943, was a pioneering electrical inventor, after whom the two-seater roadster is named.

Toyota is probably the most successful car brand of all time, taking the Japanese company from 1950s obscurity to become the world's biggest manufacturer today. In 1989, Toyota launched this new logo, consisting of three ellipses. Two of them intersect to form a kind of 'T', standing for Toyota, while an outer one encircles an empty background, suggesting the limitless opportunities available to the company.

Points: 45 **Top Spot!**

TRABANT

On the bonnet of the Trabant – the only small car available to citizens of communist East Germany until the fall of the Berlin Wall in 1989 – is a large capital 'S' in a ring. Why? The tiny cars, now collectors' items, were built in the VEB Sachsenring Automobilwerke factory, Sachsenring being the name of a nearby racing circuit, and provider of that mystery 'S' initial.

Points: 25

Over the years Triumphs used a range of logos on their cars from a globe to the slightly bizarre 'open book' design shown here. A circular decal served as Triumph's logo from 1975, when the graphic victory laurels could be found on sporty cars like the Spitfire, TR7, and Dolomite saloon. The last Triumph car was sold in 1984, so they are all classic cars today. Score for any Triumph logo.

Points: 25

TVR

These three initials are seen linked together in this simple script on the low-slung bonnets of a wide range of high-performance sports cars. The last generation of TVR was made in 2006, in Blackpool. Today, a new model is being developed in collaboration with Gordon Murray and Cosworth, due for launch in 2017. The letters are a contraction of TreVoR, from Trevor Wilkinson, the man who founded the company back in 1947.

Points: 5

The familiar logo with a griffin (half lion, half eagle), holding a flag with a 'V' on it, was designed by employee Henry Varley in 1915. It was derived from the family crest of 13th century nobleman Fulk le Breant whose London home, Fulk's Hall, became Fawkes Hall, Foxhall and ultimately Vauxhall, where the carmaker was founded in 1903.

 Points: 5

Volkswagen ('People's Car') was developed in 1930s Germany to provide the German people with affordable motoring. The resulting VW Beetle built the company post-war, and the model name survives to this day.

Points: 10

A circle with an arrow pointing diagonally out of its top right corner is the mapping symbol for iron. It was selected by the founders of Volvo in 1927, because it fitted perfectly with their intention to build cars that were extremely sturdy. Volvo, by the way, is Latin for 'I roll'.

This British make of two-seater sports cars has been on sale since 1983, and has always borne a circular logo featuring an Art Deco-style sunset. Many owners enjoy driving the cars on the road and at weekend motor sport events – and also building them, as Westfields can be purchased as a kit for assembly at home. Over 10,000 examples have been sold.

Points: 30

WOLSELEY

Lucian Milasan / Shutterstock.com

Between 1932 and 1976, Britain's upmarket Wolseley cars could boast a radiator badge that was truly unique. In cream plastic, with 'WOLSELEY' picked out in red, it was the only logo in the world that was illuminated at night. When the headlights were switched on, the logo came alive too! Sadly, this feature didn't stop the brand, considered rather old-fashioned, from losing popularity, and eventually dying out.

You may be fortunate enough to see a sports car carrying this spiky 'Z' emblem. If so, it will feature bodywork designed and built by the Italian design company. It has created special versions of such cars as Alfa Romeos, Aston Martins and Lancias. They are highly sought-after by collectors, so you might have to go to a classic car show or rally to spy a Zagato-bodied car.

INDEX

i-SPY

How to get your i-SPY certificate and badge

Let us know when you've become a super-spotter with 1000 points and we'll send you a special certificate and badge!

HERE'S WHAT TO DO!

✓ Ask an adult to check your score.

✓ Visit www.collins.co.uk/i-SPY to apply for your certificate. If you are under the age of 13 you will need a parent or guardian to do this.

✓ We'll send your certificate via email and you'll receive a brilliant badge through the post!